AFRICA

Troll Associates

AFRICA

by Francene Sabin

Illustrated by Allan Eitzen

Troll Associates

Library of Congress Cataloging in Publication Data

Sabin, Francene.
    Africa.

    Summary: A brief overview of Africa's geography.
    1. Africa—Description and travel—1977-
Juvenile literature. [1. Africa—Geography]
I. Eitzen, Allan, ill. II. Title.
DT12.25.S22   1985   960   84-10560
ISBN 0-8167-0236-5 (lib. bdg.)
ISBN 0-8167-0237-3 (pbk.)

Africa is a land of contrasts. It is made up of deserts and rain forests, orchards and grasslands, high mountains and deep canyons. It is rich with natural resources, yet many of its people are poor.

Africa is the second largest continent in the world, being about two-thirds the size of Asia. It is bordered on the northeast by the Red Sea, on the east by the Indian Ocean, on the west by the Atlantic Ocean, and on the north by the Mediterranean Sea.

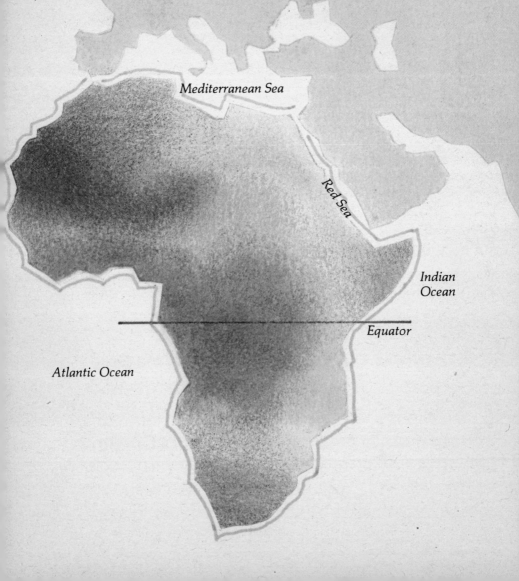

Along the northern coast of Africa—right along the shores of the Mediterranean—is a thin strip of rich land filled with fruit orchards, olive groves, and farms. The weather here is pleasant, with hot, dry summers and mild, rainy winters.

Just south of this thin strip of fertile land
is the world's largest desert, the Sahara.
Here the days are scorchingly hot, and the
nights are chilly. It almost never rains in the
vast reaches of the Sahara. But the Sahara,
like most deserts, is not all sand. This huge
desert has many miles of bare, rocky
ground. It also has many miles of pebbly,
gravelly land, as well as enormous regions
of shifting sand dunes.

Yet there are places in the Sahara, called oases, where water reaches the surface from underground streams, springs, or wells. Each oasis is a green island of trees and shrubs in the middle of the dry, open desert. The only places where people can live permanently in the Sahara are on oases.

South of the desert there is a wide band of grassland. Like the prairies of North America, the African grasslands provide good grazing for animals. The grasslands are home for zebras, elephants, giraffes, antelopes, rhinoceroses, lions, leopards, hyenas, and many other wild creatures. The climate in the African grasslands is warm all year, and there is a moderate amount of rainfall.

In the center of Africa the weather is always stifling hot, and rain falls almost every day. This is Africa's tropical rain forest, where the trees grow so thick that the sun cannot reach the ground in many places. The equator passes through the central African tropics.

South of the equator lie more forests, as well as grasslands and deserts. And all over the continent there are tall, rugged mountain chains; high, flat plateaus that stretch for many miles; and canyons tracing deep, jagged lines over the land.

Nile River

The world's longest river, the Nile, runs
north from the highlands of central Africa
to the Mediterranean Sea. The waters of the
Nile make the lands along its shores green
and rich in the middle of the desert waste-
lands. And on this rich land, civilizations
have flourished since ancient times.

In the valley of the Nile River, the ancient
Egyptians built magnificent temples, statues,
palaces, and tombs called pyramids. Many
of these handsomely decorated monuments
still stand, preserved by the hot, dry climate.

Africa's second largest river, the Congo, runs west through the rain forests into the South Atlantic Ocean. The Congo is used as a water highway through the dense forest country.

Boats on the Congo carry people, mail, and many products. The rubber, cotton, coffee, fruits, and vegetables grown on plantations in the rain forest are shipped to the coast on Congo river boats. These boats also carry manufactured goods from the coastal ports deep into the African interior.

The other great rivers of Africa are the Niger, the Orange, and the Zambezi. At the head of the Zambezi River is spectacular Victoria Falls, which is twice as high as North America's Niagara Falls.

Along with its rivers, Africa's lakes are used for transporting people and commercial products, for fishing, and for irrigation of surrounding farm lands. Africa's largest freshwater lake, Lake Victoria, is the second largest lake in the world. Only North America's Lake Superior is larger.

Niger River

Congo River

Lake
Victoria

Zambezi River

Orange River

Monkey

Gazelle

Antelope

Hare

Fox

Chimpanzee

The wildlife and other natural resources of Africa are as varied as the land itself. From the camels of the North African desert to the antelopes far to the south, the continent teems with wildlife. There are gazelles, foxes, and hares in the deserts. Monkeys, chimpanzees, gorillas, hippopotamuses, crocodiles, and many kinds of lizards live in the rain forests of central Africa. The

Gorilla

Hippopotamus

Ostrich

Lizard

Crocodile

animals of the rain forest, along with those of the grasslands, make Africa a living zoo.

The bird, snake, fish, and insect life of Africa is remarkably rich, too. In fact, scientists are still discovering new species every year. Africa is the home of the world's largest flightless bird, the ostrich, as well as more than 2,500 other species of bird life.

19

Africa is also home for the venomous cobra and mamba snakes and the crushing python. The waters of Africa hold a stunning variety of fish. There is the beautiful flying butterfly fish, the Congo catfish that swims upside down, and a strange air-breathing catfish that can live on land for days at a time. When this catfish's home waters dry up, it wriggles over the ground like a snake until it finds a new pond or river.

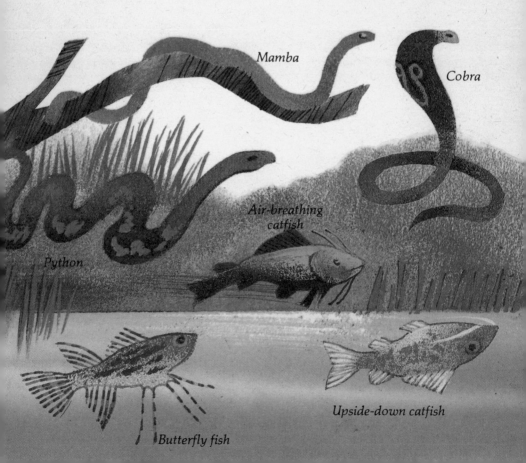

Mamba

Cobra

Air-breathing
catfish

Python

Upside-down catfish

Butterfly fish

Bee

Fly

Cricket

Moth

Butterfly

Spider

Ants

Beetle

Termites

Insects, too, thrive in the warm African climate. The land is alive with bees and flies, grasshoppers and crickets, butterflies and moths, beetles and spiders, ants and termites, and countless other species of insects.

All of these kinds of wildlife can exist here because the land has a great variety of plant life. This same plant life feeds the people of Africa. Grains, such as corn, millet, wheat, and rice, are grown in many areas. These, together with the fruits and vegetables that flourish in Africa's climate, form the basis of the diet on the continent.

Rubber, cocoa, tea, coffee, and sisal (a fiber used to make rope) also are important African crops. But these are grown mostly for export to foreign countries.

In modern times, Africa's mineral resources have become its most important contribution to world trade. The most precious materials in the world—diamonds, gold, uranium, and cobalt—are brought out of African mines. The continent is also the source of iron, copper, tin, bauxite (to make aluminum), chrome, and phosphates that are used to make fertilizers. And perhaps most important of all the products of Africa is oil.

The mineral and oil wealth is helping the economy of many of Africa's emerging nations. Modern medical facilities, education, proper food, and employment can be paid for with income from the sale of minerals and oil.

As mining and manufacturing industries expand, and modern cities are built, the old ways of Africa's tribes are beginning to change. Today many people live in modern, bustling cities. Even so, Africa is still a continent of many old traditions, tribes, religions, languages, and customs.

Some tribes of North Africa are nomads who move about the desert and grasslands all the time. They are animal herders and traders, just as their ancestors were for centuries. Many of these nomads are Moslems, who follow the teachings of the prophet Mohammed. The Moslem faith unites the people of many African tribes. It is also the single largest religion on a continent having numerous religions.

Most of the people who do not live in the cities live in tiny African villages. They live the way they have lived for hundreds of years. A village is often the home of one clan or tribe. People in a tribe have their own language, customs, and culture. And often all of the tribe members are related to each other by birth or marriage.

The tribe is an important factor in the lives of many Africans. There is a tribal chieftain and usually a council that makes rules and settles disputes. People within a tribe help each other in hunting, fishing, farming, and caring for children. For these reasons, the typical African village is more than a collection of bamboo or leaf huts. It is a very secure and comforting environment, where everyone in the tribe has an accepted place.

The language of one African tribe may be different from the languages of its nearby neighbors. There are well over 1,000 different languages on the African continent.

But the majority of the North Africans use Arabic as their first language, while Zulu, Swahili, and Hausa are the main languages of the rest of Africa. And English, French, and *Afrikaans*—a language that comes from Dutch—are spoken in many parts of the continent. These languages were brought to Africa by settlers who came from Europe.

Africa is a continent with a great variety of people, religions, climates, customs, and languages. It has modern cities with huge international airports, and it has villages where people have never seen a doctor or an automobile. It has parched deserts and steamy rain forests. It has tall mountains and deep canyons. It has animals of nearly every size and description. It is a land that is filled with contrasts of all kinds—and it is a truly fascinating continent.